they

"They"

by:
Timothy Arliss O'Brien

They

By Timothy Arliss O'Brien
Copyright © 2015 by Timothy O'Brien
Self-Published through Blurb
www.blurb.com
Cover design by Jeremy Judson Jones
Sonship.Design@gmail.com

Internal layout by Timothy O'Brien
Made using BookWright
www.blurb.com/bookwright

All rights reserved. This book or any portion thereof may not be reproduced or used in any manner whatsoever without the express written permission of the publisher except for the use of brief quotations in a book review.

Library of Congress Cataloging-in-Publication Data has been applied for this ISBN

For permission requests, write to the author, addressed "Attention: Permissions Coordination," at the email below.
timothy.a.obrien.88@gmail.com

FIRST EDITION

They

1

i. They

ii. Wife Time

iii. Town

iv. Friends

v. Talk it out; Why don't you.

vi. Diary Entries; 126, 137, and 150. Respectively.

vii. CONFRONTATION

viii. me.

ix. burn.

x. Dreams.

xi. NIGHT.

xii. TOMORROW

xiii. DIARY ENTRY 210

2

xiv. SOMEONE ELSE.

xv. GOING BACK TO HER.

xvi. Beaches.

xvii. Voice.

xviii. We will be found at home.

xix. Church.

xx. Let's move.

3

xxi. Loving you.

xxii. Long remembered feelings.
A conversation with the counselor.

xxiii. Beautiful.

xxiv. Junk mail piles up on the sofa and random words spill onto the floor.

xxv. direction.

xxvi. Stop buying useless stuff!

xxvii. Past.

xxviii. Hoping for a Cause.

xxix. Repeating the mantra taught to her by her therapist, from the results of the personality test.

4

xxx. Summer has ended.

xxxi. A letter she found from her sister to him in the third drawer from the bottom on the left-hand side of the desk in the entryway.

xxii. Understanding ourselves.

xxxiii. Time.
A journal entry made while on opiates.

xxxiv. A bottle, a party, and a couple.

xxxv. Appeased.

xxxvi. Let's make an evening of it.

xxxviii. Unexpected ending.

xxxix. Wistful Longing.

xl. In conclusion, in eulogy.

This is for all those who have held onto sanity
with a death-grip.
-T

1

I. They.

They met once.
She can't remember correctly.
Did he sigh every time she laughed?
No. That can't be right.
How do you celebrate a ten year anniversary?
It's not a special trip to the coast if one lives close-by now.
They could dance! She loved dancing.
She felt like a pout would fit her face better, sometimes.
They can eat! At a expensive hotel restaurant. Or a diner. They always liked diners. He did.
Anniversary. Celebration. Party.
Can they throw a party?
Are they happy enough?
Parties are for extremely happy people.

II. Wife time.

Shopping list

- grapefruit
- kerosene
- flowers for the flowerbed
- birdseed
- make a counseling appointment
- take meds   - don't cry
- run away
- stay
- forget about problems.
- unsubscribe from the newspaper

She hated reading the newspaper with him.
Why can't he talk to her.

III. Town
She traveled to the store alone. She hated driving.
She feared she would get lost and never find her condo again.
When she got to the store she couldn't find a place to park,
so she parked at the record store down the street and walked fifteen minutes.
She should have brought a jacket.

She had trouble deciding what brand of kerosene to buy,
And getting the nerve to get her prescription filled at the pharmacy.
She always felt the pharmacist judged her deeply, knowing what was wrong with her.

On her way to get the flowers, she heard someone calling her by name.
It was a lady she did not recognize or at least had no cognitive memory of.
The lady noticed and said,
"Remember me? From the book club? I live down the hall on the other side of the building! I find my face so memorable." She muttered.
"My mother says I have a beautiful face but my father always found it quite ordinary."
As the lady rambled, she was interrupted,
"I need to go get flowers."
This newfound friendship promptly to joined the flower excursion.

IV. Friends

"You should buy these flowers.
They are beautiful.
I think they are called xeranthemums."

Her friend had no clue what they were.

She bought them to plant in the flower bed anyway.
She was exhausted.

V. Talk it out; why don't you.

"Bringing oneself to an impasse might not be as romantic as first perceived,"
She never felt like her therapist was listening.
Is he deaf?
"I can get on board with some bandwagon mentality if my husband would talk to me more often. Or go to church with me."
"Please no shouting."
He was wrong. She didn't shout. When did she start shouting. He couldn't hear very well anyway.
Was he deaf?
It was for his benefit.
She shouted or he would not understand.

VI. Diary entries; 126, 137, and 150. Respectively.

I.
I understand.
I conceptualize.
The dream was real, they are all real.

- take more meds to stop sleepwalking.
- go to church.
- buy a birdwatching book.

Our relationship was real and the perceiving of our emotions gave us nuances.
That is what the therapist was trying to communicate. Right?

II.
Punctuating, we used to run.
From each other? Ourselves? Time?
I used to digest time as mine.
Not anymore.
Am I growing weaker over the days?
My control gives out under me and I want to fly.
Like the seagulls by the beach.
No. I want to scream.
But I don't.
Do not scream.

VII. CONFRONTATION

Her: Push me away again, I DARE YOU!
Him: You don't have to react. Act. Personalize.
Rationalize. React.
Yes.
Don't lash out so....... Ballistically.
Her: I hate that chartreuse shirt on you.

VIII. me.

She was on the phone with her sister. Or brother. Her mother? No; her sister.

"I think I'm this type of person. And then I realize I'm not. And, and..."
    "how bad is the storm there? I heard about it on the news just now,"
Her sibling interjected.
    She continued to verbally explode anyways.
"I get stoned. I get so high and still, Anxiety."
Was she crying? She couldn't tell.
"In all directions. Anxiety. AND HIGH! Where am I?"
 Lightning set the room ablaze. Visibly. Tangibly. Noticeably.
"What the hell am I even doing?"
A slight crackle responded on the other end of the line.
Had she even called anyone?
She couldn't remember.
She started the conversation over in case someone was listening.
"I need us to run away tonight. I need to be the one to get away. Do you hear me?
No one knows us or who we are. We are dream catchers. We are the runners. The hopeful, the..."
Lightning cracked and the power went out.
She went cold.

IX. burn.

She slowly doused the old shirts in kerosene. He would not even miss them. Chartreuse ablaze.
He didn't come home often this month.
She hoped it was an affair.
She wasn't pretty anymore.
The other option scared her more.
Terrified.
Petrified.
Engulfed.
Fossilized.
Engulfed.
Chartreuse.

He will be happier next month for their anniversary.
She promised herself.

X. Dreams.
No one knows her. Or who she is.
She is a dream catcher. She is a rent payer.
There is war in the streets.
Against each other.
Against all odds.
She ran away.
Looking for our destiny. Her destiny.
In rivers. In forests.
In gutters. In alleys.

It was near midnight as she got closer to her condo. Or was it four AM.
She hadn't slept-walked in years.
Ages.
Millennia.
Eons.

The homeless guy in the door stoop was smoking incense. Burning. Charred.
Like he had known the week she was having.
And it calmed us. She waited for the crosswalk.

XI. NIGHT.

Has it always been this dark at night?
I remember it being more jovial and chipper,
clippers, cosmos.
Why are we so small.
Comparatively.
Understandably?
Knowingly.

XII. TOMORROW.

The next day she remembered how they used to be in that Punk Band.
"We are musicians because we know it better than a personal craft. Our personal craft."
He used to say.

She reminded him that morning but he couldn't listen. He could only smell her.

Her perfume trailed off before she was even a block away.
She began to sing to him.
Even though she had already walked away.

"You have been my sun,
As I have been your moon.

You spark my passions.
As I engulf you in mystery. Misery. Mastery."

She couldn't remember more.
She started to make up words.

XIII. DIARY ENTRY 210

I wish I had a boat. I could sail away and gain some perspective.
Push me away, why don't you?!?
The ocean is closer than it was when we lived in Providence. Is that what you want?
You were never weak!
You still aren't, I don't think...

2

XIV. SOMEONE ELSE.

Someone else lived on the coast. It was a beautiful day in Europe. She knew that the return of the migratory seagulls meant that Summer was coming. Anything. Everything.

Years ago she had come to grips with herself. A long walk around the block had done her good. Others always gave her grief, saying "You can't handle anything."
But that was before she pulled together.

Now she was happy. Now she was free.

She watched the struggle,

The struggle of someone else,

Someone who didn't have an opportunity to get an upper hand.
Someone who would never quit fighting.
A sad story told about someone far away, who would never come out on top, but she would keep going.

Would you understand her bravery? Would you understand that people like her would need their story to be told for people like us?

There are so many people, so many stories and lives and hopes and dreams and destinies and appliances and rooms and situations.

It would be very easy to lose grip of herself again. But she lived on the coast and the seagulls had come back.

She would not lose the upper hand this summer, and dedicate herself to all those who would never have an upper hand.

XV. GOING BACK TO HER.

Sometimes if she was alone too long she feared
she was deaf.
She would close her eyes and pretend
she was blind.
She would call out "Cindy!"
And when there was no response, she would get
frantic.
Like a real mother.
Nurturing, caring,
Unbridled.
Soft. Able to cook.
Able to hold things together.

His car pulled up outside.
She wanted to lay in the grass.
She wanted it to rain.
At least he came home for dinner.
How long had it been since she screamed.
Should she cook?
Should she eat?

 It was the neighbor's car outside.
Rattling away under the dizzying streetlights.

XVI. Beaches.

"I wanna be a car family with you."
She shouted into the meadow.
The daisy looked to her inquisitively.
She had driven to the coast in approximately
twenty minutes.
She wanted to be,
    Out of this meadow
        Over the sand dune,
And   In the ocean.

She had driven 110 mph the whole way.
The whole...
Way.

The ocean scared her.
She was so small.
(Comparatively)
Speeding scared her.
She might have died.
Could have...
He was never angry enough,
When she ran away like this.

XVII. Voice.

She knew the shitty bartender at this coastal diner didn't have one ounce of sympathy for her musings but she languishly chatted on anyway.

"Traveling across a barren wasteland was not something I was keen on doing."
He asked if she was going to visit a friend.
"You can't visit where you aren't welcome. Time takes a toll on family. Ten years is a long commitment. Ten? Ten. I don't know; I've lost count. I guess that proves that the anger is real and deep.
Real deep."
"I don't think I am going to serve you any more drinks", he said.
So she went home.
Not speeding as she drove.

XVIII. We will be found at home.

Underneath the cupboard was a mouse.
She swears she saw him the other day.
She debated calling an exterminator.
But she found herself exhausted.
She started a conversation with the little rodent,
Hoping for mutual accompaniment.

This radically eased her loneliness and disease-
like boredom.

XIX. Church.

We gotta be good.
For our grandmothers and church friends.
Her grandmother would tell her.

She loved going to church.

Why do I come here?

So things won't hurt as cripplingly.
So we could be a happy couple.
So I could say "yes" to everyone, and mean it.
Because I am worth it.
So I could see that I am worth it?

To remove accusation out of my mind, if possible.
To restore my relationships.
No one can take away any of this.

My destiny can't be summed up in words.
I have set up my future to exactly what I want it to be.
I need to treat myself like royalty.
I'm convinced and persuaded that I am fine.
I'm good. I am understandable.
Making me visible to my loved ones,
Really visible.

Is this powerful?

What is my sense of reality for the future?
What am I agreeing to.
What am I creating.
What doors am I opening and paths am I pointing towards.
What am I partnering with.

I agree with everything.
It is the safest way.

I am healing.

I have eyes to see and ears to hear.
Always forever.

She had become a professional at forms of subterfuge to evade increased arguments in her home.
Another day in paradise.

I need to be a family.

XX. Let's move.

She hadn't had the "We need to move" argument in over a year.

"I'm not a stranger in the city anymore."
She shouted.
"I can walk anywhere I want but someone will recognize me."
He sighed.
"It's time to move to Vegas, a friend told me, but I said I was more suited for New Orleans, where at least if people recognize me they wouldn't want me recognizing them either."
He let out a chuckle.

They stood in silence for twenty minutes.

"I get scared that I will have to move due to a lack of awe and reverence for my city."
He didn't understand.
"Then I realize I have a different type of reverence for it."
He asked her to elaborate.

"I don't revere it as one discovers a new city and becomes enthralled by the nooks and crannies of adventuring, but I do have a reverence that the same food cart will be there week after week."
He nodded.
"Or that the same sun will set upon the city night after night. She was exhausted and it showed. There is security in sameness, and solace in familiarity."

"We can still run away to New Orleans if need be."

He said this with no commitment to improving her mood.

He leaned in to her.

"I promise I won't forget about that dream anytime soon."

She smiled.

He returned the smile.

3

XXI. Loving you.

A note left for her, from him, on the counter, as he left for a conference in Cincinnati until Friday.

There's something to be said,
About loving you the way I do.
Something to be mentioned,
As informal as lovers.
There's something in the air,
 something.
I can't catch my breath!

And if I could just stop,
And ponder you for all my life;
If I could just breathe,
And sit a spell and talk with you.

Then maybe,
I could understand,
How you understand,
The way I lose my words,
The way I lose my mind,
Every time I hear your name.

XXII. Long remembered feelings. A conversation with the counselor.

Go back to work? Wow. What am I to do?
It would be another day's choice.
To alienate, to saturate.
Standing by door alone every day, waiting for things to change.
Adjust to this kind of lifestyle?
How could it look? I don't know. Just enjoy life?
I do what I want. The real me, my truth.

This summer could be recapturing myself.
Her counselor nodded silently.

One could gain an accurate
assessment of one's condition,
owning the condition.
He whispered more to himself
than for her benefit.

Let's move on to the next thing after we "get it"
on this one.
Her counselor sounded hopeful.

"Do this 10 page personality worksheet."

Really? Why?
Bland. Balmy. Soft. Caustic.

Why did I freak out when I moved here? Why is it "my last chance" in my mind? Why is it a "one chance or else"? Why no mistakes?

Was she yelling again? She had a habit of yelling.

That mindset is making mistakes
and you cannot take anything seriously out of
fear.
He jotted down.

It's ok to live. He mumbled.

The fear leaving will kill problems.
And make life easier, he continued.
 I've screwed up due to fear, she interrupted.

Content in the long term equals continual good
feelings. Yes.
He kept writing things down. She didn't
understand anything.
Obviously. Obliviously. Methodically.
Thoughtfully.

If I incorporate myself then I will belong. I made
the team but I never played.
She exerted in a sing-song tone.

Am I devaluing myself as just a contender and
not who I really am?

Don't wanna regret and miss out.
Miss out on intentionality,
and intimacy,
and social cues,
and running away,
and being biased.
Her counselor had fallen asleep.

I'm on "my true". She told herself.
She was not deceived.

XXIII. Beautiful

A letter to her sister,
"The ocean was beautiful,
It cannot be denied that the transition
left me with an overwhelming sadness.
What's to be expected in a situation as such.
It's as though I have died
and been tragically
brought back,
finding myself with nothing and
with everything having moved on.
Such an understatement.
It's so daft how the world keeps spinning.

The coast was marvelous.

Things are finally perfect,
and I couldn't feel more crestfallen.

XXIV. Junk mail piles up on the sofa and random words spill onto the floor.

Urgent partner is needed!
This is not a dating offer!!
We see your adequate happiness,
Get remedy.
We are sending you a special greeting which we hope you will accept with a warm heart, though I have not met with you before, I believe that one has to risk confiding in someone to succeed in life endeavors.

Will you be an heir to an estate?
Do you matter to anyone?
Is your life important?
Are you real?

You can contact us.

You might be successful.

Please respond.

We can help you conquer life!

Never forget your meds again!!

Don't drown in all
The confusion
Your partner puts you through
Life is rough
But a timeshare in Italy is a great escape.

Thank you for your participation
Enjoy the fight of life.

XXV. direction.

My love,
We are together, we are alone.
We must try new things.
Together and alone.

What do you need?
Do you require a lot of patience?
We must constantly recommit our whole selves
during times of testing.
We must contain the tools to navigate,
These uncharted waters.
Contain
the tools
to navigate.
Constant recommits whole during testing.

There are not as many obstacles as one had once
perceived.
Is there a lack of focus?
And don't get started on work ethic.

What do I need? No! What do we...

Get out of my head. This angst is the proper way
to get this done. Plan, beloved, plan.

And be defensive with yourself.

Purchasing your dreams isn't realistic. Don't suspend yourself. Don't box yourself in.

What if we stop depending on people? Stop depending on people. Stop.
Constant recommits whole during testing.

Go to a concert,
steal some money,
let your passion last a year,
for something,
let impetuousness drive you,

Let this be a turning point for you.

September gives us a better view of interest and dedication.

XXVI. Stop buying useless stuff.

She always told him, he never needed a motorcycle.
He never listened to her.

One of these days...
Maybe another day.
When their song came on the radio nothing happened.
He used to take her to the jazz club and they would dance. She loved dancing.
He bought the motorcycle anyway.
She was never right.
Was her happiness important to him.

Once upon a time they were happy and they could be happy again.

XXVII.Past.

Back in high school,
She used to dip her cigarettes in cyanide she ordered off the internet.
If she was gonna die slowly, might as well do it right.
Her lipstick always tasted like charcoal.
She wore white like every day was her wedding day,
but that shit always turned brown with mud,
from running away through fields in the middle of the night.
She always pissed off people like it was her job.
But the boys still heckled her when she walked down the street,
And begged her to spend an evening at their house.
But she would always want to remain lonely.

XXVIII. Hoping for a cause.

Beneath us.
Stand late with energy.
For sake in.
Lead in transformation.
Many problems, seven of them.
Like starting an illuminati.
Maybe someone was following her, maybe she didn't understand where she was going. What she was doing. Who she was.

She needed to start looking at overcoming an overarching everything.

She always regretted killing that chicken with her grandmother. And cooking it for dinner over a kerosene stove.
It made her a bad person. A murderer. That's why she went to church.
To become a good person. A saint.

She was kind to all her crazy neighbors.
The guy down the hall would always shout at her.
She would never get angry.
She never called the cops on any of her neighbors.

A saint. The Neighborhood Saint.

This made her good person.
She was sure of it.

XXIX. Repeating the mantra taught to her by her therapist, from the results of the personality test.

I love and enjoy myself.
I have healthy boundaries.
I am passionate about things.
I allow myself to contain secrets.
I value and respect others in relationship to me.
I value and respect myself.
I allow myself to experience things.
I love myself to be a gift to others.

Do I allow myself to be a gift to myself?

My emotions can connect me to others.
I find myself confusing.

Well that's confusing. Comforting? Consoling?

I shall learn how to take care of myself.
I need to know my needs.

I need to understand better what this exercise is about. Where is the reasoning behind this?

Do I even understand myself well enough to be able to understand myself well enough to be able to understand myself?

Well this this has been helpful.

4

XXX. Summer has ended.

She left a voicemail since he should be out of town until Thursday.
"What a dark summer we are having,"
Or was she on the phone with her father?
Her memory eluded her.
"summers have not seen,
What we are seeing now.
If everything ends tonight,"

"Heaven forbid," he sighed as he listened.

"Should there be anyone left to forgive?
I don't think you understand," she screamed.
"There is nothing that could remedy.
There is nothing to let go of this.
There is nowhere to put this,
It finds our insecurity and..."

He will call her in the morning, he figured.
      After she took her meds.

XXXI. A letter she found from her sister to him in the third drawer from the bottom on the left-hand Side of the desk in the entryway.

To whom it may concern,

It's with a heavy heart that I put in this letter to you in regards to her.

I can assure you she is over you. And her therapist has done all he can to help her recover and she's finally starting to recover and has made great strides over the past time in particular.

Time to better understand recovery isn't it.

Personally I feel you had to have never encouraged her to go off her meds in the first place.

I know the stressors she has up there do not help. The condo is too small. It is too far from the coast. And the possibility of losing your ability to provide for her.

It has been very painful to watch her go through what she's been through.
Anyone under normal circumstances would have lost it.

I am to understand that the stressors up there do not help her
in the slightest.

She genuinely cared about you and was trying to make amends.

For heaven sakes the stressors alone.

She's waking up
She's realizing
Especially right now while she is still healing.

I am thankful for you.

It has been a growing experience for all of us here.

I think she has learned a lot and hopefully will not repeat.

She is starting to get on with her life again.

Enjoy making new friends,
Sister.

XXXII. Understanding ourselves.

Truth is truth regardless of our experience.
I am like a sleeping infant in this season.
Giving out roses season.
I love speaking in tongues.

XXXIII. Time. A journal entry made while on opiates.

Why has November come to us

so early.

The smoke rings exude June,
But
    my
        Heart...

To us,
NOVEMBER
        has come,
on Time.

XXXIV. A bottle, a party, and a couple.

I need to find something to do.
It's my own fault I'm bored.

Words can be a liberating part of where you want to go.
Looking back on the past I realize I was a shell of a human.

A refill of wine sounds lovely. After which I shall pick this up where we left it.
Remember to smile. Constantly smile.

I went from party to party in those days, looking for an excuse to ruin my life.
I wish I could study myself from back then. Like a lab rat.
I could watch, and have a "fly on the wall" perspective where nothing could hit me personally.

Even when conversation ebbs and flows, continue to talk. Is anyone listening?
Make them listen. You can be as interesting as you want.

Just watch from afar.
Adrift.
Inept.
Socially.
A mess.

By the time I leave this party I will have it all figured out.

No matter how many people get left behind.

XXXV. Appeased.
A journal entry on a napkin from a truck stop coffee shop.

Maybe I am a goddess.
Maybe my anger must be appeased.
The old and decrepit must meagerly think over their lives,
Coming to terms with the waste of the rich and the melancholy happiness of the poor.

"How can we appease her?" They ask.
"Can she teach us about existence?" They stare.
The bottle never drank itself and the idiot didn't believe his own lies.

Trucks keep on going by and hair keeps on growing.
We mustn't give in to the idiosyncratic whims of our mothers.

"Don't worry about her," they'll say, " appeasing her never does any good..."

XXXVI. Let's make an evening of it.

Absolutely missing the shit out of him while he is gone.
Bitterly hating every moment he was around.
Cooing to herself softly to ease the ringing in her ears.
Drinking an entire bottle of wine by herself.
Effortlessly losing track of time,
      while planning to redecorate the entire condo.
Forcibly screaming at herself in the mirror for what seemed like hours on end.
Guests always felt at home when she tended on them hand and foot.
Helping herself to another bottle of wine since the hostess never had it so easy.

It is irritating how quickly people leave and are uninterested once a party is over.
"Jovial time, pal!" Said his friend on the way out the door,
      as she wondered if she would be happier having married him instead.
Kicking herself for thinking such thoughts.

Lovingly crawling into bed together.
Marriage was such a facade.
No one understood her unhappiness.

Openly she would talk about it from now on.

People would respect and admire her with their empathy.

Quickly she jumped out of bed at this new realization,
Realizing she had now fixed every problem in her sphere,

She was ready to start her new life.

Tiptoeing back to bed, she crawled under the covers, careful not to wake him.
Understanding her new role in life, she drifted off to sleep.
Vehemence followed her in her sleep.
Wonderful dreams of a perfect life followed her.
The xeranthemums in the front yard withered and died overnight.

Youth and happiness would be on her side once again, now that she had chosen to live.

XXXVII. Your eyes.
A poem written to her newfound love, with whom she had loved for the past ten years.

The color of kelp
Floating in the sea.
The color of moss
On a rock in a storm on the coast.
The color of a forest
During a crisp spring twilight in May.
A patch of grass
Just freshly mowed,
A neon light
Showing where to go.
A reflective street sign,
During a midnight disorientation.
The perfect color.
The only color.

XXXVIII. Unsuspected ending

Motorcycle. Trouble.
Car trouble.
Fast.
Loud music.
Intoxication.
Misunderstanding.
Running.
Fast.
Shouting.
Tripping.
Spill.
Miscommunication.
Misdirection.
Broken glass.
Yelling.
Headache.
Screaming.
Flames.
Rolling.
Directionless.
Visionless.
Quietly.
Hurt.
Rejection.
Absolution.
Pain.

Loneliness. No, distraught. Yes. Distraught.

Why must they kill their darlings, she muttered.

And just like that she was alone.
Very alone.
Always alone.
He was gone.
Terminally.

XXXIX. Wistful longing.

The collection has started.

I keep people in my life like one collects tea cups in a cabinet.

You have left a mark on my life, an impression that has changed me.
Looking to you has gained me strength. And now I have courage to conquer.

Now I am brave. You have shown me courage. To be brave. Oh to be brave. A change has happened and what once was is now refined.
***
You may stay. There's no future in my stars without you. And now I'm brave.
****
To be brave. Oh to be brave.

Attention attention. I think this calls for some publicity. I think we have lost him. He isn't here and he's oh so quiet.

XL. In conclusion, in eulogy.

She processes her grief of His wise departure in pen, in poem.

forgone.

"Forlornly,
Move across turbulent time.
Friendship connects,
But stays connected."

A seagull passes overhead.
    She continues,

"They aren't gone. They ain't forgotten."

The sun must have set an hour ago, or more...

"They are just gravely missed."

    No one was there,
to clap.

- "Amen."
        She sighed.

The end.

TIMOTHY ARLISS O'BRIEN

Lives in Portland Oregon,
and was born and raised
in Oklahoma City, Oklahoma.

When he isn't writing fiction, you can find
Timothy writing classical music.

Milton Keynes UK
Ingram Content Group UK Ltd.
UKHW010025040324
438776UK00002B/426